The Business Guide:

Proven Techniques to Launch and Expand Your Business

by

Oscar T. Milton

Table of Contents:

INTRODUCTION

One of the most thrilling and rewarding experiences you can have is starting a business. But how do you get started? There are numerous approaches to starting a firm and numerous crucial factors to take into account. Follow this thorough how to start a business guide to help remove the element of guesswork from the process and increase your chances of success. I'll guide you through every stage of the procedure, from developing your business concept to making it a reality.

Chapter 1

What is a business, and why should I have one?

An organization or enterprising entity engaging in commercial, industrial, or professional activity is referred to as a business. A business's goal is to coordinate some form of economic production (of goods or services). Businesses can be for-profit corporations or nonprofit organizations working to advance a social cause. Businesses vary in size and scope, from small, local enterprises to enormous, global conglomerates.

A person's efforts and operations to produce and sell goods and services for profit are also referred to as "business."

Business planning is frequently necessary before activities can start. A business plan is a formal document that specifies the strategies and plans the company will use to accomplish its goals and objectives.

Since business owners may need to get licenses and permits and adhere to registration requirements in order to start legal operations, determining the legal structure of the company is another crucial consideration.

In many nations, corporations are regarded as juridical entities, allowing them to acquire property, incur debt, and face legal action.

Operations in Business

To make sure that everything runs smoothly and successfully, businesses engage in a variety of operations and activities. Employees can operate completely within their own area of expertise by grouping these operations. By concentrating on a number of important variables, including accounting, finance, production, research & development, and sales, these operations support the overall business structure.

Accounting- involves keeping track of all financial transactions for the company and assisting management with resource allocation choices.

Finance- Managing the company's money, keeping track of its capital requirements, and assessing the potential effects of borrowing money on the health of the company are all aspects of finance

Manufacturing- is the process of creating goods and/or services to satisfy customer demands.

Marketing- Identifying consumer requirements to produce goods or create services

Research and Development: Professional analysts assist the company in staying competitive.

Sales- Increasing revenue and closing sales are the company's constant objectives in order to maintain profitability.

Variety of businesses

Services, manufacturing, or business sectors are the three areas into which businesses often fall. The nature of a business is defined as the classification of a company's line of operations and products. Each type of business focuses on finding unique ways to satisfy customer wants in order to be profitable.

Service Business- Provides customers with intangible goods (services), such as labor or expertise.

Manufacturing enterprises- Produces goods to be sold to other businesses using raw resources.

Retail businesses- Sells manufactured goods to clients directly.

Why should you launch your own business?
The internet offers innumerable sources of advice, and the connected world of today has created millions of new markets for small business startups. The internet has also made it possible for business owners to network with their peers, learn from their errors, and use the successful decisions of others as a roadmap for their own journeys.

If a nine-to-five job isn't for you, it could be time to build your own ladder, go at your own pace, and leave your impact on the world. Here are some compelling arguments for starting a business right now if you have a great concept or a burning passion

i) Being your own boss

Rather than beating your head against a wall every time your employer makes a mistake, take the initiative and make your own judgments. It's natural for people to want to avoid taking chances, if you don't take risks, you'll always work for someone who does.

If that idea terrifies you, it's time to start preparing for your entrepreneurial path. Here are just a few advantages of working for yourself:

Greater control- You determine how money is spent, the type of workplace culture you desire, and the standard of work to be produced.

Flexible hours

Gives you complete control over when and how much time you spend working.

Diverse learning

Exposes you to every facet of starting a business, from financial management to health and safety.

ii) Describe your job in detail

If you believe you have a variety of important talents, starting your own business offers a way to make the most of your abilities.

You shouldn't be scared to perform grunt labor since, as an entrepreneur, you'll play a variety of roles in your company, especially in the beginning. You'll frequently be in a variety of roles, such as manager, marketer, therapist, and receptionist.

The following are crucial entrepreneurial abilities:

Business management abilities Such as the capacity to multitask, delegate, and make judgments that will affect the health and profitability of your firm,

Leadership and Teamwork skills In a small business, you'll likely be the team leader and supervisor.

Customer service abilities will help you build relationships with your clients and forge joint ventures.

Strategic thinking and planning abilities are required to stay competitive, achieve your business goals, and expand your market reach.

Financial skills are required to ensure that you understand and control the financial side of your business.

Branding and Networking before hiring someone to take this over, your brand will be promoted and grown via networking, marketing, and branding techniques.

iii) Switch your passion into profit

Since starting a business is dangerous, it's critical to keep your motivation in mind when times are rough.

Almost a third of small enterprises fail in the second year, and 20% fail in the first. Since the early years of a firm are challenging, maintaining your passion is essential.

When in doubt, try to remember these advantages of establishing your business:

- Self-actualization: You get to create your own vision rather than follow someone else's
- Watch it grow:You get to watch your creation develop from an idea into an empire.

- It's personal: You get to devote your time and energy to something you love.

iv) Boost your potential for income.

Maybe the income at your current job isn't what you'd like it to be, or maybe you have a side passion project that has the potential to grow into a successful full-time job. In either case, you'll need to put in the time to make it a business.

Entrepreneurs are prepared to put in 80 hours per week if it means avoiding working 40 hours per week for another person.

Although you could initially face financial difficulties, stay motivated by remembering the main goal of starting in the first place.

make other people's lives better.

Starting a new company gives you the chance to hire and train people who may not have previously had the chance to find a respectable job. Additionally, you get to have a significant influence on society.

Accept failure and use it as a learning opportunity.

Some companies fail because they produce subpar goods; others do so because their goods are released at the wrong moment. Most businesses fail either due to a lack of demand for their goods or services in the market or because they run out of money.

It becomes obvious that failure is something to be faced head-on and learned from when you consider that 90% of start-ups and 75% of venture-backed start-ups fail. Here's how to go about it.

Take accountability:

Take responsibility for your error and don't place the blame elsewhere.

Try the humor test:

Can you laugh at the last mistake you made? Recognize why you made the error and how to prevent it in the future. If so, it's likely that you've thought it out and moved on

v) Become an authority/expert

Create your own opportunities rather than waiting for someone to offer you the chance to excel at something you love.

Avoid falling into the trap of dogma, which means accepting the conclusions of other people's reasoning.

Develop expertise in one area by determining your passion:

Find an interest you are passionate about, as this will make it easier for you to continue with it after work.

Finding the time- Practice, practice, and practice some more is the greatest method to become an expert, whether this is done by experience or learning through online business courses.

maximizing every opportunity- Accept anything that challenges you, whether it is large or tiny, paid or unpaid.

Chapter 2

Techniques for Starting a Business/Feasibility Studies

It is obvious that there are many factors to take into account when beginning a business, but with a carefully thought-out plan and the right methods in place, you may achieve your business objectives.

Apply the following tactics:

Making the ideal business plan

A business plan is required if the venture will need investors or loans. This demonstrates that a plan is in place and details how the idea will be carried out, as well as the kind of profit the entrepreneur hopes to make. A business plan is a crucial road map for a company's growth; this practical document typically includes a projection for the next three to five years. Additionally, it offers a framework for the direction the company plans to go in order to improve its reputation and increase profits. As a general rule, these plans should include an executive summary, business description, strategies for advertising and marketing, competitive analysis, and acknowledgement of real competition within the field. Various types of business plan programs are available to take the guesswork out of what needs to be included. It should also include development goals, management and operations strategies, and any information relevant to the company's finances, such as launch expenses, cash requirements, and profit projections.

Make a Fantastic Marketing Strategy
Without effective marketing, the company will not succeed. Without marketing and advertising, the business will remain hidden and unprofitable. Customers and clients must be aware that the company exists. A grasp of your target market and a competitive analysis of where the company will stand in the market are

both important components of a solid marketing strategy. Knowing your customers is essential; be aware of who they are, what they want, and how they behave. Make a list of the people who could benefit from the product or service, then figure out how to target them with advertising efforts. Thoroughly examine both demographics and psychographics, and then decide if there is a real need for the product or service among these customers.

Calculate the finances.

Although there are many ways to finance a company, the financial requirements of doing so are frequently a barrier to getting started.

- **If at all possible, carry on working even as you launch your new enterprise**

Verify there are no conflicts of interest (particularly if the new business offers the same goods or services as your current position). Maintaining a payroll can significantly speed up the time it takes to launch a new company.

- ## **Add a second source of income while waiting**

Offer your skills and services as a contractor or freelancer to save money for the company and reduce the need for future borrowing.

- ## **Cut back on expenses**

Plan your costs today to reflect the fact that the company will need money. Change spending plans to include more savings. This may sound obvious, but even a small bit here and there might significantly alter the outcome when applying for a loan.

- ## **Look into loan options**

You can be eligible for loans that you aren't even aware of, so do your homework and be well-prepared for loan talks.

The financial parts of starting a business should go more smoothly if all factors have been thoroughly studied and business and marketing plans have been made. It's crucial to keep in mind that launching a business is challenging, but it is possible with perseverance and confidence.

Study of Feasibility for Small Businesses

A small company feasibility study is a thorough investigation and financial analysis that advises on whether to proceed with a product or business idea. Estimates of things like revenue, expenses, barriers, and technical difficulties are included in the study.

Feasibility Study for businesses

Businesses typically undertake feasibility studies to decide whether their concept or product is worthwhile. It's one of the more time-consuming and expensive methods of evaluating a business idea.

A study can take weeks or months to prepare, depending on the idea's intricacy and scope. Business owners can carry out feasibility studies on their own with the aid of templates or applications. However, an entrepreneur can employ a specialist to create the study due to the extensive research and challenging financial estimates.

Feasibility studies give all the information and make a strong recommendation on whether or not it's best to proceed, but they do not make the ultimate choice.

A feasibility study is used by small business owners to avoid making the costly error of launching a failed venture. A study can be used to inform strategic choices, such as deciding whether to-

- Launch a new company
- Open a new factory or store.
- Expand to a new region or market
- Change the product lineup or strategy.
- Make a sizeable investment in new technology
- Enter market that is already crowded or competitive.
- Put some of your personal money into a project.

Each of the elements listed below will be utilized to a different extent depending on the project or business. Depending on its focus, the feasibility study's structure may change; you might have a section for each of the following subjects:

Summary: This is an executive summary of the project and company. These are the ultimate conclusions.

Demand: A market analysis identifies the market's demand for your service or product in the sector you intend to target. Even if you run a physical storefront, you should take internet factors into account.

Technical questions: What equipment, software, or tools are required to build your enterprise or product? Will you develop the technology, purchase it, or rent it? The facilities, including the layout, shelves, offices, and manufacturing area, are also included in this part.

Logical issues: This article discusses vendors, price plans, exclusive agreements, and franchised product contracts in relation to logistics. Obtaining materials, shipping finished goods, or managing internet components like an e-commerce website are a few examples. Problems with location can be found here.

Legal questions: Do you require licenses? Are there any restrictions or rules to take into account? What about negotiating environmental, historical, or legacy issues?

Marketing strategy: This paragraph will provide the most detailed definition of the target market: How would you respond to their needs and how would you approach them?

Staffing requirements: How many workers will you require? What are their credentials? How much does the average person make in your area? A sample organizational chart and a discussion of which of your present employees might shift jobs to fill open positions can be included.

Scheduling: This section outlines a timeframe for completion, financial milestones, and physical project milestones.

Financials: This section will include an opening day balance sheet that details the total assets and liabilities on the first day of your business, along with estimated expenses and potential profits. This financial information allows you to estimate your return on investment (ROI).

Return in investments: Starting or growing a business is pointless if you don't expect to get your money back. A feasibility study predicts when you'll make money, what it might be, and how much it might be.

Analysis: You'll witness debates addressing issues like: Does it sound plausible? The sources seem reliable. Do we need to take unusual data points into account? Examine potential hazards as well.Which worst-case possibilities are most likely, and how likely are they?

Recommendations: This provides go-or-no-go advice and deconstructs particular recommendations based on the key components. It might provide alternatives if the project is not possible.

To sum up-

Feasibility studies can cost several thousand dollars, but they can prevent you from losing millions of dollars due to bad business decisions. They conduct research into the technological, financial, and operational facets of a new business or product proposal. The research examines the information and makes recommendations regarding whether or not you should pursue your project or idea and how to increase its likelihood of success.

Chapter 3

Overcoming Business Obstacles and Growing Your Business

A business's expansion is no easy task. Over 65% of businesses fail within the first ten years of operation. A weak turnover or even closure might be caused by poor marketing, unstable financing, or a lack of customer demand, but these shortcomings can be lessened with a sound growth strategy.

What is a growth strategy?
A growth strategy is a strategy to boost a company's size and worth. It involves establishing your strategy for defeating your rivals holistically and determining the most effective means of doing so. It also applies to practically every aspect of marketing, as well as to other divisions like sales or product-led growth.

Three components make up a strong strategy: a diagnosis of the problem, a guiding principle, and cogent action. Diagnoses take into account the full procedure, researching your rivals, and comprehending your standards and metrics. Customer marketing analysis and knowledge of how to increase audience engagement are part of this. The method and desired destination are defined, expressed, and communicated in a well-constructed guiding policy, together with the steps necessary to achieve each milestone. The coordinated action then moves on to the finer points, such as tactics, operations, and governance. All three parts and their constituents will be taken into account in a sound growth strategy.

Business expansion strategy

Growth strategies today have a slightly different appearance and a more modern philosophy. The popular Four Ps may be familiar to you if you've previously studied growth. Product, placement, promotion, and price are these. Whereas audiences, channels, and pricing are the center of the Four Ps.

The Four Strategies for Growth

On the basis of this, four different growth plans are suggested. The following are the four primary growth strategies:

Market penetration

The goal of this strategy is to boost sales of currently offered goods and services in order to gain market share. You can achieve this by luring clients away from your rivals and/or ensuring that your current clients purchase your goods and services more frequently. This can be achieved by lowering prices, increasing promotion and distribution assistance, acquiring a competitor in the same market, or making minor product improvements.

Market development

This refers to boosting sales of currently offered goods and services in untapped markets. Market expansion entails analyzing how to expand an existing market or how to sell a company's current offer to new markets. Different client categories, such as industrial purchasers for an item that was previously marketed only to homes, new areas or regions of the country, and foreign markets, can help achieve this.

Production development

The goal of product development is to introduce new goods or services to markets that already exist. Product development can be used to expand the offer given to current clients in an effort to boost sales. The following methods can be used to obtain these products: Investing in the research and development of new products; Purchasing the rights to produce someone else's product; Purchasing the product and "branding" it; jointly developing products with another company whose ownership requires access to the firm's distribution networks or brands

Diversification

This refers to the introduction of new goods or services into untapped markets. The riskiest tactic is diversification. It entails the corporation offering brand-new goods and services in a fully untapped market. Additional categories of diversification include:

Horizontal diversification: This refers to a company's decision to acquire or create additional products with the intention of marketing them to its current clientele. Current customers might be interested in these new products even if they are technologically or commercially unrelated to current products. For instance, a business that formerly produced notebooks might now introduce a new product into the pen industry.

Vertical diversification: It refers to a company's entry into its suppliers' or customers' markets.

As an illustration, imagine starting to offer paint and other building supplies for use in your company's home and office renovation work.

Concentric diversification: It is the development of a new line of products or services with technical and/or commercial similarities to an existing range of products. Small manufacturers of consumer goods frequently employ this form of diversification when, for example, a bakery begins making pastries or dough products.

Conglomerate diversification: It is the transition to new goods or services that do not share any technological or commercial connections with the existing goods, machinery, or distribution systems but may appeal to brand-new client demographics. The high return on investment in the new industry is the primary driver of this type of diversification. Large corporations frequently use it when seeking strategies to balance their non-cyclical and cyclical portfolios.

How to overcome Business Obstacles

As a business owner, you may face a number of difficulties, but the good news is that you may find solutions to them. Read through the following list of typical business challenges to get a better understanding of what to anticipate and how to overcome them:

Giving Up Your Current Job

It is sensible to continue working in your current employment while also running your new firm in its early phases. This approach is a surefire way to keep your steady income while pursuing your entrepreneurial interests. But there will come a time when it must be your top priority if you are serious about starting your own business. Unfortunately, nobody will be able to advise you on when to leave your day job. Instead, you must choose the point at which your business endeavor is sufficiently promising to offer the level of financial backing you need. This may appear to be a dangerous choice for many business owners. The good news is that changing jobs is becoming a more frequent occurrence, so quitting your office job won't leave a huge gaping hole in your resume. Instead, you can only say that you founded your own firm if you ever wish to return to your prior profession. If your company's venture is successful, you won't second-guess your choice.

Making Use of Repetitive and Ineffective Methods

If you have ever run a successful marketing campaign, you are already one step ahead of the game. Remember that a successful business does not necessarily follow from a successful campaign. Failure to diversify one's firm, especially when things aren't going well, is one of the largest challenges faced by business owners. Contrary to popular belief, switching up your marketing and communication tactics is one of the best ways to guarantee the survival of your real estate business.

Business owners should think about new investing techniques in the long run, in addition to expanding beyond lead generation. If your wholesale firm has been reasonably profitable, it might be time to think about flipping your first home or getting a rental property.

Feeling Overwhelmed Following An Error

Despite how cliché it may sound, everyone makes mistakes. It's okay if you lost money on a deal, missed a significant networking event, or passed up a business opportunity. The best course of action is to see every challenge as a teaching moment. It serves no purpose to keep thinking about things that could hinder the development of fresh business opportunities. Instead, alter your viewpoint and consider how you may get better in the future.

Absence of Motivation

Do you find it difficult to recall your "why"? Spend some time exploring your surroundings for ideas. This can entail looking up comparable organizations for fresh inspiration or simply thinking back on your long-term objectives to rekindle your motivation. Business owners frequently experience motivational slumps, especially if they haven't closed a deal in a while.

Going through Tunnel Vision

Celebrate all of your victories, no matter how tiny. You'll be more likely to remember to value your company and all that it entails if you engage in this habit. Many investors occasionally experience tunnel vision while looking for offer after deal. This way of thinking can be detrimental because it might cause sloppy actions or even a lack of motivation. It could be time to review your objectives if you have been having trouble with tunnel vision.

Do You Have a Staffing Problem?

A common challenge for novice business owners is taking on too much responsibility. After all, if you're used to doing everything yourself, it can be challenging to delegate chores. To prevent burnout, it is essential to learn how to assign certain tasks to others. Even if you wanted to, you can't accomplish everything yourself. Start your search for small-scale jobs you can outsource by studying virtual assistants. At the same time, start networking in your community to meet other real estate experts. You'll be able to put together a strong team over time.

You're Losing Your Brand Identity

It will take time to develop a strong brand identity, and you'll need to make adjustments as needed. The most crucial thing to remember is to adhere to the mission statement of your company. From there, make an effort to maintain consistency across all of your messaging and platforms. Always keep in mind that your actions determine your future actions. Your company's future success depends on building (and sustaining) a strong brand.

Have Old Contacts

When did you last make changes to your contact list? As a business owner, you should continually expand your network. The best way to make sure you continue to be involved in your community and generate new leads is to do this. There are a few ways to do this, like joining neighborhood Facebook groups, going to networking events when you can, joining a neighborhood investment club, and showing up at public events to get your name out there. As a business owner, almost everything you do can be viewed as an opportunity to expand your network of contacts.

Loss of Focus on Sector Trends

Staying on top of industry changes is a challenge that many investors encounter. Regardless of how long you've been in business, staying on top of current real estate trends is essential. Keep an eye on local rivals and cutting-edge technology that could benefit your company. Keeping up with developments in the stock market and the global economy is also a smart idea.

It's not difficult to keep up with market trends; in fact, you can incorporate some research into your everyday routine. For instance, if you frequently check social media, try following accounts that are relevant to your business to get updates throughout the day. Another smart move is to routinely keep an eye out for any changes in your neighborhood market.

Chapter 4

Improving Your Business and Setting Boundaries

Business improvement has been defined as the process of a "thing going from a state that is judged to be worse to a state that is perceived to be better, typically through some kind of action or intervention meant to bring about such improvement and change".

Business Improvement Methods

- **Marketing**

The major goal of this kind of business enhancement is to boost sales. Whether it be done by boosting market share, running promotions, enhancing the customer experience, or using any other typical marketing technique,

- **Process Improvement for Businesses**

Business process optimization aims to improve operational procedures and increase their effectiveness. There are countless examples of process improvement because each organization has its own distinctive procedures. One popular strategy is to automate manual tasks whenever possible to free up staff time for other tasks.

- **Quality Boosting**

The phrase "quality enhancement" actually means what it says. It's about raising the standards of various parts of your company. This could involve making your product or service more competitive, but it could also mean enhancing the standard of your company's internal operations, such as practices or processes.

- **Improvement in Management**

As you might have imagined, management improvement is concerned with raising a company's level of management. A straightforward example of this would be leadership development. However, it might also involve shifting the distribution of authority, such as giving management more internal control.

- **Capital Upgrades**

Capital enhancement centers on increasing the amount of money put into the company.

Examples of capital improvements include building new offices to accommodate additional employees or purchasing an existing business. It alludes to investments made in the business to make it better.

- **Technology Information**

This kind of enhancement focuses on modifying or modernizing the technology that your company now employs. Examples of this include modernizing cybersecurity technologies to safeguard the security of customer data or modifying internal processes to increase productivity inside.

- **Changing the company culture**

This sort of business improvement, also referred to as organizational culture improvement, focuses on enhancing corporate culture. Regardless of whether they are consciously aware of it or not, every company has a unique company culture. When there is a lack of company culture, it has a significant impact on employees' well-being and productivity as well. Changing the organizational structure of a firm frequently centers upon changing the company culture. to eliminate hierarchical structures in enterprises most frequently.

What are the limits/Boundaries of a business?
Business boundaries are just restrictions you set up to allow you to operate at your peak capacity, effectively service your clients, and still have energy and relax.
You can manage your client interactions and safeguard your energy with the aid of these tips. Setting limits proactively helps you stay away from issues like exhaustion, misunderstandings, and irate customers.
The advantages of establishing limits in business
Being a business owner means you are in charge of managing your customer relationships as well as safeguarding your personal resources. When you do this-

- You are able to best utilize and protect your spiritual, empathic, and intuitive abilities.

- You are more productive because you are able to better manage your time and energy.
- By being transparent, you improve your client connections and foster trust.

Chapter 5

Business Marketing Strategies

Expanding brand recognition and creating a bunch of qualified leads that convert to sales are the goals of marketing. Getting the word out might be difficult for a small firm because of reduced visibility and limited resources (like budget or time). However, there are important tactics that can assist you in scaling the marketing initiatives of your small firm.

A marketing strategy that's ideal for your business can offer direction as you scale, whether you're battling with a constrained budget, the time constraints brought on by having a smaller workforce, or even a lack of direction.

These strategies are crucial as you promote your organization and raise funds for it:

Be aware of your audience

Consideration that "anyone" is your customer
What is driving people to choose a product to
buy? How will it appear if they are successful?
Understanding these factors will enable you to
create communication that connects with
listeners and persuasively supports your
solution.
Start by considering who you want to
collaborate with among your current clients.
Next, begin the process entering the mindset of
your ideal customer.

Attract attention to your value offer.
There is no compelling reason for a consumer to
patronize you if there is no distinction between
you and your competitors. Your value
proposition will set you apart from competitors
in your industry and convince prospects that you
are the service they should choose. What are you
better at than anyone else in your field? This
provides a strong case to be made.

**Remain focused on a single goal or set of
goals.**

When learning more about the field of marketing, you might have observed that there are countless possible paths to follow. It's tempting to tackle everything at a go and build a complex machine in the belief that you've taken care of everything, but it's also simple to take on too much.

Decide instead where the greatest impact will occur. What is the biggest marketing blind spot you have that is preventing growth? Set performance objectives and records around that one important area and concentrate your efforts on the strategies and actions needed to meet that one objective. When you've made more progress toward that one objective, you can increase your efforts or change your strategy.

Profit from short-term opportunities

Begin spartanly. It's crucial to realize ROI sooner as you scale. You will then have the momentum and money flow to work on more ambitious projects, long-term strategies, and sustainable growth models.

Because you won't get a return on your investment as quickly as you'd like, strategies that take time to grow (like SEO) are poor choices for your main objectives. Put some of your eggs in other baskets if you have enough resources to start there.

You can discover that paid advertisements will provide you with an immediate return on investment if you have proof that people are using Google with the intention of acquiring your specific product.

Expand on what is effective
Once your efforts are up and running and you've tried a few different things, pay attention to the statistics. You can learn what's working from this. It's a smart idea to increase your reliance on tested revenue-generating strategies as you scale.

Recognize the influence of current clients
The obstacles with acquiring a new customer is typically five times greater than that of losing an existing one. This means that after they must

have purchased from you, you shouldn't stop marketing to them.

Know your prospects for cross-selling, upselling, and recurring business. Your current clients already know, like, and trust you since they have already transacted with you. If they had a good experience, they would be likely to work with you again if the need ever arises.

You should still delight your customers even if the necessity isn't present (in situations where it's a one-time buy with no upsell opportunities). Word-of-mouth is very powerful and most times cost-free

Make use of free advertising resources

Speaking of free advertisements, it's important to remember that you don't need to increase your costs by using gadgets because you've committed to a specific objective and range. When possible, use free promotional tools; only invest in paid tools if you are very sure that they will significantly boost current operations or performance.

To improve your online presence, build a website

One of the most outstanding things you can do for your small business is building a professional-looking website. Here, you will describe your company's background, services, location, and methods for contacting you.

It is a channel you will always own (unlike other platforms that may change policies or go in and out of style), and it offers the capacity to send traffic from advertising and other marketing initiatives in addition to being a location to send organic traffic.

Likewise, your website is more than just a static brochure. By learning how to convert traffic into leads and transforming them into sales, you have the opportunity to turn it into a 24-hour salesperson.

Self-promotion on social media

Social media is a wonderful tool for businesses because thousands of potential clients use different platforms every day. You can use social media to interact with potential customers, increase brand recognition, and advertise your goods. Why wouldn't you want to be recognized where your prospective consumers hang out?

Capitalize on word-of-mouth advertising as a marketing strategy.

As was previously noted, pleasing clients can significantly affect your company, particularly in terms of repeat business and word-of-mouth. Your customers will be more likely to leave reviews, give testimonials, and refer you to friends if you give them a wonderful experience. Because of this, it makes sense to gauge client satisfaction and motivate repeat business.

Buy advertising

You should invest in short-term strategies as a small business because organic traffic takes time to develop. Advertising strategies that target customers with high intent are excellent for achieving quick wins that help launch your goals.

If you know that your target audience is looking for your product or service online, try out

Google Ads. If not, you might think about using social media advertisements. You can pique the attention of your audience with properly targeted ads and a sufficient number of impressions.

Conclusion

Starting a business is not as easy as it looks on pen and paper, but with determination and the ability to put the right techniques into practice, you will definitely be on your way to the top in the business world!

9 798358 341951